May this book honor the many teachers who have shown graciousness, shared their gifts of learning, and humanity with me. I give thanks and feel blessed by all those who have supported me over the years in continually meeting and waking up to my humanity.

"Take a moment and breathe as you step into this reflective heartfelt wisdom filled new book by Rik Center. Rik effectively creates a pathway for each and every person, a framing that invites the reader into a personal self-discovery that offers a reflective moment toward personal growth. Rik muses in ways that make the journey into self-awareness; positive, fun and that can be immensely rewarding. I've admired Rik and his work on so many levels for years, plus for full disclosure, I get to be his cousin. I'm honored to serve as a reference for this exciting new book."

~ Scott Marshall Brandon, Co-Author of Imagination First, Co-Owner of Litrof Consulting and over 25 years tenure as Executive Director of Education at Lincoln Center.

if you can't change your mood change your mind

mindful reflections toward self-discovery

by Rik Center

ISBN 978-1-7332493-0-0

First Edition
Centerspace Publishing

Contact for Rik Center
www.mindfulnesscare.org
www.rikcenter.com
rik@mindfulnesscare.org

Cover Art by Paula Egan ~ Cover Design by Carla Dal Mas.

Preface:

This unique book of thought provoking reflections offers the reader a rare opportunity to look at ourselves without judgment, without negativity, and with a potentially transforming clarity. Rik Center shares his subtle yet inspiring observations that offer building blocks toward a compassionate way of reflecting upon daily life. We are shown that self-discovery happens when we make a personal choice to pause, look within ourselves, and be curious. From the very first page, Rik encourages us to slow down and meet our truer nature; one that knows that the opportunity for change indeed exists within each of us.

Rik shows us from his own journey there is a richness in the space between the breath and thoughts; a precious pause that affords a joining of the heart and our inner wisdom. Take for example these conjoined 18 words found within the covers of this book: "We can ask ourselves...if looping over and over, chasing scrambled thoughts has ever lead toward inner peace?" So simple yet so profoundly true!

There is no preaching or finger pointing here, but rather simple (or perhaps not so simple) messages that, upon reflection, can change the trajectory of one's thoughts and beliefs. Readers are treated to nuanced quips, quotes and poems that are woven with artful humor, yet possess a directness that asks the reader to bring in more of their own personal inquisitiveness. So relax, read and absorb Rik's wisdom from over 30 years of a mindfulness practice and see where it might lead you.

Grant E. Young, Ph.D

The waves rippled gently toward the shoreline
seeking nothing other than to be a wave
movement flowing into stillness.

A destination rising from the depths of the waters
to a pin-pointed meeting with the white sands
they become the lapping still waters upon the shore.

Allowing for each moment of the ebb and flow
to meet the sands of time...where nothing is clung to.

By opening the heart to mindful reflective teachings, we gain
learning...from the learning, we gain compassion...
from compassion, we gain wisdom.
When these three aspects blend, we become the architects of a
new future in how we respond to the nature of life.

We are not changing the characteristics of pain, loss or joy,
though transforming how we interact with these experiences.

INTRODUCTION: The Path Begins Here…

This book is a collection of quips, quotes, and poems that have emerged from a personal spiritual journey which began many years ago and continues evolving to this day.

My path into self-discovery began early in life while attending a private Orthodox Jewish school. At times the religious teachings combined with home life, family illness, and watching people in public felt confusing with a sense of contradiction. Then the heavy toll of loss had to be dealt with when my mother passed away. Depression and teen angst were part of life while navigating the world and being with others.

At the age of 26, I crashed headfirst into mother earth from a hang-gliding accident. Struggling to heal this emotional-physical embodied-pain, I began to recognize that our heart-mind-body is interconnected. Our every thought and response has a cause and effect on everything that happens in our lives. I realized how the human mind resists what it does not want or like, creating inaccurate stories to avoid deeper unresolved feelings. You can visualize this as a horse wearing blinders. A good part of the landscape is hidden while only a fraction of the surroundings is seen. I call this the "stingy mind."

In this book, I share the reflective nuggets, the subtle "aha moments" that have come out of my mindfulness meditation practice guided by a profound Buddhist spiritual, psychological education. Cultivating a reflective meditation practice has helped me slow down enough to consciously witness my own thinking and acknowledge the pains of the mind/body with nonjudgmental compassion.

The path of self-discovery has built within me a healthier relationship to the natural ups and downs of life. Recognizing that early on in life, I began to depress uncomfortable feelings when the world was not how I wished or I felt unheard. If we defend unskillful habits into our adulthood that ignore our humanness, how can we ever expect real change to happen? If we suppress or deny feelings of discomfort, we are creating an act of pushing away.
Who are we pushing away...ourselves!

The "stingy-mind" keeps us blindly cut-off from our ability to recognize that comfort and discomfort are the very bookends that allow us to feel whole. The practice of mindful-awareness is not about thinking we should not feel or grieve; it's recognizing that we do.

May these subtle nuggets of reflective wisdom that continue to support me be a positive resource for you, the reader.

You might wish to take a moment to pause throughout the book and reflect. This pause is the space where the inner heart of goodness and the mind of awareness expand to become part of this new self-discovery.

You see...
It was love the moment I came to be
a mystery not for the eyes.
Oh you know...yes, it's everywhere!
Walk with me my friend.

The world can be seen
from within a delicate awareness.
Here I am...Here you are.

Reflective Groupings:

1. Here and Now
2. Inner Awareness
3. Being
4. Consciousness
5. Awakening
6. Mindfulness The Way
7. Practice, Practice…Practice
8. Reflective Motivation
9. Self
10. Thoughts
11. Listening
12. Kindness
13. Discernment
14. Self-Compassion
15. Life
16. Non-Suffering
17. Letting Go
18. Awakening II
19. Nature
20. Spiritual Reflections
21. A Stroll In The Forest
22. Conclusion
23. Reflective Poems On Loss

Here and Now

The mind looks left, the mind looks right, searching how to make everything just right. This non-stop search is tiring. We begin where we are, where we always are, right here. The mind will rehash the past or even live in a future that has not even happened. This does not change the fact that our physical body of awareness through sight, sound, smell, taste and touch is always present in the "here and now."

———————————————

Where else can it be?

When we resist life and the present moment of our experience, we are not responding to the actual experience. It seems we have to keep learning this over and over.

Life is not about living in the thoughts
we believe should happen.
Life is about living in the experiences
that are presently happening.
Reflecting and learning from them.

Transform painful, confused experiences into...
compassionate, caring moments of present moment connection.

To be present, we must acknowledge where we are.
Why allow the mind to ignore this fact?

Our thoughts can often keep us caged...
Imagine being taken to a prison cell where the keys are placed
on a rack only two feet away outside the cell-bars that can
easily be reached.

Now the keys are quite close...yet the mind is far away.
Our thoughts run wild with a sense of entrapment.

How can this be happening?
How can you do this to me?
Come back and unlock this door.
I deserve to be treated better than this.
What's going on here?

The key to our freedom is right here.
Give the mind a moment...pause.
An opportunity of stillness allows for clarity.
Only we can do this for ourselves.

Sense this moment...this body of experience.
All is noticed here...your life.
Why look elsewhere?

The key to unlock the mind of discontentment
is within ourselves.
When the realization arises that there is no actual key,
we are liberated from the belief there was ever a lock.

A memory of the past is a thought happening
…in the present moment.
Thinking of the future is a thought happening
…in the present moment.
Both thoughts are creations happening
…in the present moment.
Awareness of this fact allows for a truer response
…to the present moment.

The awakened body
of sensation…
Finds clarity in the present.

Stop for this brief moment…be still.
Notice your body…sense this one breath.

Who are you now?

Who did you believe you were 11.5 seconds ago?

The sound of the wind does not know of its sound.
The air lifting the bird to soar into its emptiness does not know
of its emptiness.
Flight is not even known by the sky.
Even so, all is one in being the nature of what is.

Inner Awareness

Inner awareness is about oneself. It's not me trying to get inside someone else's head to change their thinking. It's recognizing what is going on within ourselves within our thinking. We observe thoughts. Recognize feelings. They are changing experiences that string together the moments of our life.

It's amazing how much time the mind will spend trying to change a past experience, not recognizing true change happens in how we reflect upon experience.
Let go of this other illusion.

Clinging to past experience in the present moment
ruminating over and over
sets up future moments of
living in a compulsive discomfort.
We are all bigger than this.
Do not fear opening the mind.
Why hide from the possibility of inner peace?

What is this concept of looking inward?
Notice we have both light and dark thoughts.
People often struggle with their thinking.
We might ask ourselves…what is the fear?
Thoughts are always changing.

Release these thoughts of either or…
If this is me…then am I really that?
If I am that…how can I be this?
If I'm that, then I'm not this.
If I'm not this or that
could I be nothing?
If I am nothing
could I then be…this and that?
Is self the light?
Is self the dark?
The mind continuously loops itself into creating
something where there is nothing.

There is only you, my friend.
Sit now…sit quietly.
Be with all your heart.
No judgment here…
No this, no that.
No light, no dark.
No self, no other.
Nothing…
There is only you, my friend
Sit now…sit quietly.
Be just you, with all your heart!

All we have to do is be present
for this moment and the next.
Life will be felt and love will be found.

Let's acknowledge that we are human beings.
Being is in the moment;
a human, being in the moment.

Notice the body of experience.
Nothing to become and nothing to let go of…it's that simple.
The mind thinks there is something we must work at to
become present.
Is that whacky or what?
Just be present…it can't happen any other way.

Learning from the past,
we are able to live more skillfully
in the present.

Present moment awareness is here and now…
Where else could it be?

There is nothing wrong with daydreaming
we might just over do it.
Then wonder why nothing is changing in our life.

The breeze of life pulses through us.
If we hide it is not from the past,
though from the present.
If we run, it is not to the future
but to our past.

What shall become if we stay?
Stagnation, perhaps not...

No place to go but here.
No place to be but here.
Be still...
As life unfolds itself into consciousness.

Be the gardener of your life.
Tend to the soil of aspirations
nothing more, nothing less.

The breath is an experience of the moment.
Don't ignore this…

Being

In being, we pause the striving to become, which is a never-ending future of needing to become this or that.
Being here, being present in this moment of time…is the only place where we are.

———————————

Don't practice waking up…practice being present.
Don't practice becoming enlightened…practice becoming present.
Don't practice being perfect…practice being present.
Don't practice practice…be present with practice.
It's about what awakens within us.

We don't become aware of the present moment by striving.
We become aware by letting go.

This moment is the place where life is happening.
Is there a willingness to adjust how we relate to the moment?
Are you willing to consider this?

The future becomes the present
which becomes the past.
Then it's gone, just as it started.
All of this is happening simultaneously.

Mind…where is the mind?

When doing walking meditation repeat the mantra…
"I don't have to be anybody right now."

We don't awaken in the past.
We don't awaken in the future.
We are only awake in the present moment.

Consciousness

Recognize the experience of thoughts. They naturally arise then pass away all on their own and are in constant flux. Conscious awareness is not a clinging to absolutes, it recognizes harmful thinking that looks for absolute truths.

The DAD mind always believes it's right.
If we see life through the lens of the DAD mind,
what else do you believe will happen in our relationships?
Other than...
D... Disagreements
A... Arguments
D... Disputations

We can ask ourselves...
If looping over and over, chasing scrambled thoughts
has ever lead toward inner peace?

Stop taking the hammer of negativity to yourself;
It doesn't work.
Stop using the hammer of negativity towards others;
It doesn't work.

Be of no mind...
What does that mean?
Don't think about it.

We can be of two minds:
The 'all about me mind' or 'the curious mind.'
Which one creates more ease in your life?

Views, thoughts and opinions
Views thoughts and opinions
Views thoughts and opinions
Should be's and should not be's.
It should be this.
It should be that.
Views, thoughts and opinions
On and on and on and around it goes.
Views, thoughts and opinions…
Let me off this un-merry go round.

The spirit is true and free
when the mind is ready to surrender.

The mind can be a gift beyond imagination
or a trap…
Taking us into a tunnel of the heebie-jeebies.

When coming to understand the depth and simplicity of reflective presence, the compassionate heart takes precedent over cravings and aversions.

As the mind softens…so goes the body.

The stingy mind constantly attaches to analytical viewpoints of opinion making.
This delusional habit keeps us from meeting our good heart.

If you can't change your mood…change your mind.

In responding to what others express we can ask ourselves,
what might be the intent of my response?

I believe we all understand that if the mind goes over the same
thought again and again, this becomes our emotional state and
the physical feeling of our bodily experience.

Oh, "You didn't know this…?
Or you've been choosing to ignore this reality?"

Awakening

*Eyes can see, ears can hear, the nose can smell, the mouth can
taste, our body sensations offer touch awareness to the world.
Make the distinction between what our senses show us is the
present moment versus thoughts that want to believe something
else is happening. Don't ignore the clear awakened mind.*

I've come to realize true knowing is beyond knowing.
"Oh my…what do I do now?"
I don't know.

Practice repeating "don't know" to every thought,
see if a "self" arises.
Does a demanding "this is right and that is wrong" appear?
Perhaps a more spaciousness may arise within the mind.
This is quite different then repeating, "I know."

The mind attaches to the personalities of our
unresolved anxieties.
We might even defend these feelings
believing this is who we are.
These emotional states actually have us believe
that whatever thoughts we are experiencing is the truth.
Be careful…these anxious personas
create disingenuous beliefs and harm
toward oneself and others.

When the mind constructs a self
which our thoughts often believe must be defended
uneasiness becomes a daily occurrence
not the self-calm we seek.

Be the observer of thoughts and feelings.
Be the knower of these ever changing conditions
not the believer in them.

What's the experience of the body and mood when choosing
not to cling to viewpoints and opinions?

Be aware of non-judgment,
a non-clinging to self-assumptions.
Notice how the body experiences less judgment.
Yes, it does feel better, I know.

If we respond to life experiences with the pause of discernment.
We no longer leave out the mind of wisdom
which becomes a movement toward releasing false fears.

Emotions are not us, we experience them.
With a bit of awareness and wisdom
we see these emotional personas are intolerable
tyrants trying to rule the roost.
Shifting perspective means readjusting.
That's not a bad thing.

Don't hide from the mind's shadow
awaken to it with awareness.

The way of one is not the way of two
The way to two is not the way of three
The way of three is not the way of four
And yet when one, two, three and four come together,
They are the way.

Become the knower...What happens when the world is not
meeting your needs and desires?

Grasping at the unattainable is fruitless.
Empowering wisdom is possible.

It takes the release of the victim we carry inside
to find that patience and courage will arise.
Enter into the stillness of mind.

May the gaze of the moon graze the heart of awareness.

Beyond the bone and body lies a mystery.
Yet we can only explore the mystery through
the bone and body.
The knowing and unknowing of oneself.

Consider this:
Is it possible a core of our thinking derives from certain
survival-based instinct patterns?
Many of these patterns perpetuate our anxieties,
yet we defend them.

I don't say this lightly
if I've not understood this for myself.

Tell me…what does your heart want for you?
Let's not forget that change is possible.

Mindfulness This Way

Look this way...no, not that way.
How often do our thoughts keep looking around for others to
change so we may feel better? This unquenchable desire for
everything outside of ourselves to be just right only sustains
perpetual discontentment. Mindful awareness is the wake-up
call.

Mindful awareness...where?
Mindful awareness...who?
Mindful awareness...why?
Mindful awareness...it's about time!

Don't think about practicing mindfulness; that doesn't work.
Don't think about meditating; that doesn't work either.
Both of these sound like wonderful aspects to have in our life,
though if we only think about them
they are not being experienced.
If we are not practicing them, we are not living them.

When the heart asks you to notice it…
don't ask why?
You have feelings…quit believing you don't.

Like all moments, feelings come and go.
Acceptance is the moment of experience
and the path to change.

Mindful awareness offers the opportunity to let go of
conditioning that does not serve the good heart.

How we reflect on a memory…
determines how we experience the next moment
that's arising.

Mindful awareness is a choice.
A pause to check in with ourselves.
For myself, I've learned the mind
is quite capable of making up anything.
So I have to say to certain thoughts…
"You can't stay inside all the time,
you have to go out and play."

Just like when mom scooted me out of the house as a kid.
I had to go outside, get active and release the restlessness.
Mom was pretty smart; she knew what was needed.
Now my mind will occasionally laugh at itself
and will go out and play all on it's own.
It's a lot more fun than the alternative.

Mindfulness is often described as
being in the present moment.
Yet here and now is always changing…
Figure that out?

Mindfulness…the patient pause.

Mindful awareness is not something we have to get.
It's a natural openness that arrives from curiosity.

We are capable of releasing the mind from clinging
to unskillful thoughts.
Mindful awareness offers this to us.

Don't be afraid to look at suffering habits.

Just as the Red Sea parted
when Moses and the Jews exited Egypt.
Opening the mind, allows us to see
further than what we believed possible.

Thousands stayed behind in slavery
and would not follow Moses to freedom.

This is like the mind.

Many are willing to go beyond...
for some this is too frightening.

Sadly, they stay behind.

Practice, Practice...Practice

Change does not happen so easily, just because we wish it would. A mindful-meditation practice is like this too. We have to put ourselves into the center of everything we experience, to understand our part in creating the inner world of how we experience life.

A mindful meditation practice supports a path to clarity.
A gift we offer ourselves and share with others.

When the realization of sitting on the cushion is
the arrival and willingness to sit.
We then know the blowing wind as just wind.

Meditation: doing nothing, though much is happening.

In practicing meditation we learn to quiet the mind.
Thus, allowing in a spaciousness
for the compassionate heart to open.
This is not knowledge gleaned through books.
It's a wisdom that arrives through connecting
the mind with the heart.

In finding wholeness
we de-condition our thinking...
Go beyond who or what you believe you are.

What might happen if we give up the idea
of thinking we know what others are thinking?
Knowing all the conditions that cause anyone
to respond to experience as they do?

What might happen if you found out that 99.58% of everyone's
thoughts have nothing to do with you?

Could we handle this?
Would you allow yourself to live a happier life?

Opening to a deep love of self is
not found in the constriction of a created self.
Rather, it's an understanding of who we are not
which liberates the wounded self from its unskillful patterns.

The truth of imagination is that it's beyond imagination.
Imagine that.

Spirituality…might it be an experiential body knowing
and not an intellectual exercise of rights and wrongs?

Thinking we need more becoming; such as
…more becoming a something
…more becoming a somebody
Forcing our way into
…becoming someone.

Have you noticed how miserable you actually are?

Our need to become more…
is connected to our need to survive.
A sensing that we are not dying.

So, we make beliefs out of actions
which were based on previous actions
which were based on a desire to feel that I'm somebody
doing something that others will notice
in seeing that I'm a somebody.

Oh my!
Let go of that foolishness,
it detracts from your beauty.

You smiled, I could not see.
You laughed, I could not hear.
You cried, I could not listen.
You died, I could not watch.

It was me who was uncomfortable.
It was myself whom I feared most…
it was not anyone else.

When thoughts overcrowd the mind
notice where you are in the present moment.

Awareness of sight, sound, smell, taste and touch
are very helpful.

Finding ourselves right here…not having imaginary thoughts of
where we are and what the mind believes is happening.

Listen deeply to this body of bone & flesh
it teaches us about suffering and joy.

Don't hide…allow yourself to sense this day.
Feel the aliveness of this moment without judgment
though through the mind of compassion and gratitude.

Reflective Motivation

*Without the curiosity to reflect on our thoughts or impulsive
reactions as to why we see life and others the way we do. We
are left with little possibility for change and inner peace.*

Motivation sets our intentions into being.
Have you noticed how motivations produce
the continual outcome of cause and affect?

It was a blind man who helped me understand
the wisdom of the heart.
It takes a courageous mind to look inward at itself.

Children close their eyes to taste the snow and rain.

I too learned to shut my eyes...

To feel the earth, I have no eyes.
To taste the fruit, I have no eyes.
To know myself, I have no eyes.

It has taken many years to notice
the blind man was always me.

A self-righteous sense of anger
is a false sense of power-identity.

We are the ones who walk through the doors of time
from knowledge to dust.
No matter how relentless the passages are...
they lead to wisdom
then back into ignorance.

Finding the way out from the dark jungle of despair
we notice the path becomes the friend.
Oh so wise...Oh so caring.
How could the mind forget?
The goodness of a smile appears when the heart
allows the doors of compassionate kindness to swing open.

Has there ever been anything really closed or open?
Perhaps it's just the mind
playing another one of its tricks.

Sadness within can take over a
good heart and joyous body
feeling numb to all.
Then we cry...
Who am I?

When living in constant judgment and comparison,
the mind becomes worn-out from all the inner turmoil.
Do we have the courage to quit identifying with this type of
false thinking?

Self

*If thoughts are constantly changing, our moods come and go
and the body never stays the same. What is this self we
constantly defend? Might we stop making ourselves so
miserable?*

Self…where is it?
Self…what is it?
Self…who is it?

Perhaps it's time to let all this self-ishness go,
and just let the self be.

The breath within is found in the present moment.

Why make an ever-changing life so solid?

The mind will find a way to justify itself
in many situations, even if harm is caused.
It may be very painful to ask a person
to stop and look inside themselves
to notice what fears might be hidden away.
A created self-deception in the name
of a self-defensive stance that may
cause harm to self and others.

How do you see me?
Am I the dark cloudy storm
or the new baby
you hold gently in your arms?

Could I be the dust
that settles in your eyes
causing them to tear?
Or the lover
that caused you to shudder?

We see others as we are.
Through the lens and stories of
our personal history and experiences.

Learning about ourselves through interactions
with one another offers clarity. Allowing
opportunities of change to become possible
versus old impulsive habits deciding our choices.
The lived experience is an individual uniqueness.

Asking someone to see the world
as I do and to think as I do…
Is like asking a bear to be a fish.

The spirit is true and free when the mind is ready to surrender.

Why do humans make an identity out of stress?
This is not denying there is unease in life.
This is something everyone experiences.
It's just not who we are, it's what we experience.

In the choice to view others through personal unresolved
fears and angers, we leave them no way out from being
persecuted by our emotions.
The world is seen through the distorted lens of discontentment
that is unresolved within ourselves.

Can we say a thought or an emotion is really me or mine when
it's always changing?
Curiosity allows us to discover
that thoughts are unstable and not a real self.

We're often working hard to become someone.
Not realizing what we are working hard at
is the wanting to be noticed.
It's a societal suffering to live this way.
Could it be the one person who really needs to acknowledge
ourselves is our self. If so, quit ignoring you...

Be curious what might happen when the self quits trying to
make a self that needs to be noticed.

Self-awareness is a practice of reflection around our thinking.

Have you noticed how personal thoughts
might even treat us unkindly?

Begin to reflect on thoughts versus continuing to pick them up
when they act unruly; creating chaos and unkindness.

You're not who you think you are
and you're not who I believe you are.
I'm not who I think I am
as I'm not who you believe I am.

Inner peace does not happen when we run around
telling the world how it should see me.

The mind did not to want to see the truth.
The body had a feeling of wanting to sleep.

Ultimately, the inner alarm clock began ringing.
Wake-up…stop avoiding!

Let's be a partner with the decisions we make toward life
versus shutting out and shutting down.

Stop putting faith in idealism; begin to have faith in yourself.
Then ideals begin to have a more balanced path forward.

Fluctuating emotions are not something we need to protect
or push away. Offer them a little kindness.
Allow these feelings to move through us
so they expand the heart of wisdom.

Who is this me I need to defend?
What is this me that needs protection?
An organic body of minerals, muscles, emotions and ever
changing sensations.
With this type of understanding everything changes.

Thoughts

Troublemakers they can be when we believe them to be truthful.
Thoughts are not who we are, they come and go.
Yet, many people believe they are their thoughts.
How is that possible? We can reflect on thoughts, then decide
which ones are useful or not.

We learn by recognizing patterns within our thinking,
not by identifying with them.
Perhaps more to the point.
There is no need to act out from negative,
impulsive thoughts we'll feel badly about later.

When a thought arises, why believe this is something that must be acted upon? Pause for a moment, allow it to cease and lose the impact of its energy.
Then see if it's useful or not.

We are not the personalities of our anxious thoughts. Those old beliefs and habits just keep the good heart dampened down.

Superstitions, prejudices and biases should be recognized for what they are.
This is quite different than creating an impulsive life from these misguided beliefs.

With mindfulness and clear understanding, we see emotions
arise and cease.
They dissipate and change often.
Attaching to the impulse of unruly, emotional thoughts
allows them to become a personality.

When believing this is who we are,
common daily occurrences often start being seen through the
lens of either good or bad.
Thoughts go into… "I'm good, I'm bad"
or "you're good, you're bad."

Does this way of thinking really make anyone happy?
Of course not!
The only result possible is living with an un-easiness.

Recognize over-thinking…don't think about over-thinking.

Choosing to enter into a therapeutic process of healing,
acknowledges how tired we are of reinforcing unhealthy habits
that derive out of self-defeating thoughts.
Allow yourself to become dispassionate toward emotional
attachments that continually cause distress.

Listening

*True contemplative listening allows us to pause
our conditioning to blurt out opinions without forethought.
Without the ability to cultivate reflective listening skills, how
can we recognize assumptive thoughts?*

Listening…to who?
Listening…to what?

Do I even know if I'm listening?

Are you listening to me?

If the mind is too busy thinking
about what it needs to say next.
Could we actually be too busy to even
notice what is being expressed?

Listen, shhh…come closer.
Is this not who we are?
Laughs, smiles, tears, fear, anger and joy.
The cawing of the hawk,
the calls of thirst or hunger.

Listen…really…please listen.
Come closer…
Can you hear it?
There is a silence which leads us back to everything
where we no longer need to become one or the other.

Do our words bring about connection or divisiveness?
Could the answers we often wish for
not be found through demanding speech?

When letting go of how things need to be…
How might we then respond?

Stillness surrounded me
like a shadow beneath the willow tree.

The darkness of night moved forward
to share its evening solitude.

Inside this body of flesh and bones…grew
stories of the past, the present, and the future.

Knowing this…the stories began to quietly subside.

Kindness

Life is not so easy at times. Kindness toward others and ourselves changes everything. We have more space to recognize negative thinking habits that close off the heart of goodness.

———————————————

True generosity is understood when we expect nothing in return when offering kindness.

When the heart of goodness sends out loving-kindness toward others and ourselves for living a human life of experience…the sky and ocean become one.

Compassion means I'm capable of being bigger
than I ever imagined.
Compassion teaches me about all the fears
we hide within ourselves.
Compassion demonstrates what it is like to be human.
Compassion caresses my anger and hurt with a gentle touch.

Compassion strengthens my spirit when others are suffering.
Compassion comforts me in times of confusion.
Compassion allows me to cry when I'm feeling hurt.
Compassion teaches me about love.
Compassion allows my heart to open and breathe.

Compassion understands I may veer off the road occasionally.
Compassion will dust off my trousers and tend to my scars.
Compassion is a resting place for an overburdened mind.
Compassion allows for healing.

Be kind and patient toward yourself.
The goodness of compassion can be found everywhere
if only we are willing to slow down so it can find us.

Compassion just is...nothing else.
Here, take some of mine...there's more where this came from.

A life weaved of kindness and compassion
will meet...
Whatever mystery may lie beforehand
opening its doors gladly.

Whatever challenges are confronted
will be conquered.

Whatever mountain stands in the path
will not be high enough...

For the heart ultimately reaches toward love.

A confused, reactive mind creates pain.
Being kind and wishing good for ourselves and others is not the
delusional mind...
It is the only mind we cannot afford to live without.

The kindest way of listening
to an attached fearful mind is through
the goodness of an open heart.

Remember when feeling blue think of the sky,
how expansive and wonderful she is in all her forms.

The weather teaches us about life as it nourishes the earth.
Be kind to your storms…embrace your sun.

Every time we smile
A flower blooms
A new baby is born
And a thousand hearts embrace compassion!

The more we cultivate the inner wisdom
of a compassionate heart…
there is less of a desire to cling onto
pains of our past.

One of the kindest acts we offer ourselves
is not chasing all the conversations in our head.

Especially thoughts that seek to change bygone experiences.

Stop trying to build a new past…it won't work.
Be the architect of your new future.

Discernment

If we have a willingness to observe our thoughts, notice how often the mind of judgment and comparing like to jump in. Mindfulness that utilizes curiosity allows for the bigger me to notice the smaller me that so often makes everything "all about me."

Truth...whose truth?
Truth...what is truth
Truth...where is truth?
Start with yourself...

Recognize how much we don't know
and how much the mind makes up.

When tasting a truth, it tastes like nothing else.

Truth is always within.
Who has the courage to accept
the strength to surrender
the humility to sustain?

How often does the truth rest
inside every breath
hidden away
for only those who can see
a whisper upon the lips
of those who choose to bite
into the forbidden fruit
called life.

May I see you from the inside out…
and caress you from the outside in.

Self-love…have we not pushed it away long enough?
Self love…why believe a healthy life happens by ignoring this?

Set aside the crazy stories the mind is making up;
they're not real truths.

Seek inner peace that renounces negative narratives.

Don't put the teacher on the pedestal.
Be inspired by qualities that resonate with you
which have arisen from their learning.
This makes them human, not a deity to be worshipped.

From my hand to your hand
From my lips to your lips
Our eyes lock together
Our minds entwine
Begin the began

We may have many lovers…
Yet, who is this ultimate lover that has been so desired?

It's you of course, silly…
Where else could we expect to find the true heart?

Open to the vulnerability of the ultimate lover.

Inhale your spirit,
find the amazing you inside.

There's a deep love of self that is unknown to most
people, just a foot or two beyond imagination.
It's beyond desire for worldly objects
or the need for praise or blame.

When we come directly into contact
with this heartfelt experience
serenity and peace of mind
become our friends.

Could we learn to love ourselves so deeply we
stop pulling the trigger of harm or utter
hurtful words upon another?
Understanding these unkind acts destroy
oneself within the process.

Self-Compassion

How could we expect to understand the ultimate act of goodness that is beyond ourselves if we have no kindness toward ourselves? Berating oneself with negativity never leads to happiness...we know this.

Water flows
Fire heats
The body disintegrates
This is life

Stop being so aversive to uneasiness...
Start being more compassionate toward yourself.
The human body needs the hand of kindness.
Pushing away hurts and fears...fighting with them
typically builds emotional stories of self- negativity, guilt, and
shame.

How often you kept calling my name
though I turned away…wandering to and fro…
I could not see.

Barely able to lift my feet from this mud,
not knowing any better.
I continued slogging through the muck and mire.

Oh yes, there were many moments of glee,
rancorous behavior and
shouts of wonder.

Though my mind continued to dwell
in the cavern of dark…

Until one day I did look up
and saw your glorious smile in the sun.

Dear God, it was here that I found
your message of love in the streets of life
from the alleyways of judgment
to the back-roads of ignorance.

Sitting by the curbside on this day
was a very old young man.
He reached out from under his tattered garments
with a cupped hand and crooked smile.

This time I chose to look into those eyes
and not turn away.
Thus I began to cry.

The face may not have been familiar,
though the eyes were mine.

I knew the sad stories, fears, and depression they held.

Gazing upward I am no longer
able to ignore your smile.

You have taught me that a river of tears arrives
from within an ocean of compassion, so that
we may stand on the deck of this ship
called forgiveness and love.

Shadows are born from within the light
just as rainbows arrive from the dark stormy sky.

In life we must nurture our souls the
same as we nourish our bellies.

Embrace your shadow...
that too needs your love.

You who are the shadow within the shadow
entering each moment as we do
witnessing life as if it were a silent prayer.

You who are beyond the sight of our eyes
and the moisture of our tears
when in pain you become the holder of our suffering.

You rejoice in all of life's creation
and yet, when we look for you...
You are the shadow within the shadow.

Never heard, nor seen, though always present.

Your essence is one of love
a taste that lingers long after death.

You are the lover...
who remains in the ethernet of time.
The shadow within the shadow.

Sometimes we just need a guiding hand or a little support
to help us see beyond our stuckness.

I have walked so many miles
at times I need to cry.

Having lived so many lives it feels as
though the ashes of eternity have
slipped through my fingers.

If I must shiver from doubt within…
it is not for me to seek an answer.

You have come to me
like a whisper sitting upon the lips
of a lover speaking so silently
only the soul will hear.

Perhaps a tear is what humankind fears most.
For you see, I too had been afraid.
Yet, I continue walking through the fire of life.

If not for this heart to look within…how
could compassionate wisdom arrive?

I could not be me if I did not traverse this path and
you are the chosen one to see
and you are me.

Life

*Might we be so busy looking to create a life, we miss whatever
is happening...is our life. Life is every moment of whatever
is happening. Utilizing self-reflective awareness we are able
to notice how we are actually meeting ourselves
in the moment of experience.*

Life...whose life?
Life...what is life?
Life...what stories have you made up about life?

Clinging to a desired illusion of life
is based upon the perception of a false self,
which distorts the perception of life and
the continued illusion of this false self.
Stop doing that to yourself.

When the mind allows life to empty out
begin to notice…
How much richer your experiences become.

It is not who we meet in this life.
It is in the awareness of how we
experience life with others
that show us our life.

Testing the waters of life?
We are in it and it's all around us.
Why ignore it?

Sail boldly in this ship called life
Invite in the spray of water
In fact, fall out of the boat a few times
Who are you now?

Confusion rains chaos…
on all those believing
this life is solid in
thought and form.

If we are willing to look at our discomforts…
the false ego attached to false perfectionist ideals
might be relinquished.

Live life with more curiosity…
find the joy and awe that is all around you.

Human beings are perfectly imperfect.
Please…laugh, cry and ponder.
Be present in this moment and the next.

Our journey through life is a solo one,
yet, it is not taken alone.
When this is understood
the mind will become unshackled.

Are you able to recognize
when too much striving
becomes a hell realm?

Be present with the touch
Be present with sound
Be present with your eyes
Be present with the sensation
Be present with the heart

For it is here
where life will be found.

We could ask ourselves...
Are we willing to arouse the effort it takes to find
the freedom and inner peace that we so desire?

That is not just an occasional moment of calm clarity
but a true quality of equanimity that leads to wholeness.

A willingness to look beyond habituated patterns of the mind.
Are you willing?

If we allow it…life can be an open space of possibilities
or an endless list of blaming excuses that bind us to the past.

The body is a bridge between birth and death.
How one chooses to walk across this expanse
will be the experience of our life.

Even though the bridge may be shrouded in fog at times
it does not mean the bridge does not exist.

Allow for tears…
They awaken us to this glorious spirit called life.
Embrace them…don't hide from them.

Notice that life is a chain-reaction.
A continual process of moments linked
together within a continuous causality
of momentary experiences.

A reaction to the action coming
from choices made out of previous actions
all arising from thoughts about ourselves.

Thus, creating a compounded moment of me
which is forever changing.

There were stories of the past, the present and the future.
A cry was heard springing out
like a tiger on its prey.

The cry was my voice...

Wailing forth the song of life!

Life is not so easy…it's in constant flux.

How this flux is met…decides the vision we overlay
onto the world, ourselves and others.

Non-Suffering

How often is there a wish of our present moment experience to be different? Could there be an over attachment to the desire of wanting experience to be other than what it is versus responding to what is really happening? Responding from a state of aversion leads to discontentment, confusion and of course suffering. The path to non-suffering is recognizing this aversion. We pause to utilize the wisdom of our heart.

To understand we are all worthy of receiving grace
we must release past judgments of self and others.

Forgiveness: Relinquishing self-suffering.

When uneasiness arises…be the observer.
Watch the discomfort as an object of experience and
become curious…unless you enjoy feeding irritability?

Acknowledging we live in a body of aches and pains
with a limited timeline.
Asks of us to accept what it means to live in a human body.

Believing in something we are not
begs the question…
Where will inner peace be found if we push ourselves away
from the reality of our humanness…
Why keep doing this?

The minds greedy desire for a life that has no discomfort only
leads to perpetual discomfort.
A belief that discomfort should not exist
is a condition that gives rise to the anxious-mind.

What would happen if we learned to meet
un-comfortableness without judgment and more kindness?

Desire for absolute safety is a societal neuroticism.
It's not wrong…it's impossible.
We build a trap that has no way out.

The kindest way of listening to an attached, fearful mind
is through the compassion of an open heart.

Fear rejoices when his voice is heard.
It is in this place he feels most loved,
for you dance his dance and sing his songs
Say no…
I beg of you…
Tell him no and begin to notice;
there are no notes in his music
or rhythm in his movements.

He will fade from view and you…
You, my friend, will shine more
beautiful than ever before!

If we are living life in fear of death
a reality no one can avoid.
What might we be bringing into this present
moment of our aliveness?

Letting Go

Fear of change can be emotionally frightening, yet the fear of growth can often be scarier. Why not be curious enough to challenge and sit in the fire of our fears? Allow the natural wisdom of the physiological body to move through and beyond this emotional upheaval...so the possibility of calm and joy may arise in your life.

Letting go...of what you ask?
Letting go...of who you ask?
Letting go...stop asking and let go!

Don't be afraid to let go.
Do not let fear of the unknown stand in your true path.
Soar into the arms of the universe
where your true inner spirit will come alive.

Enjoyable times will appear…
Notice that moments of discomfort change.
They always do.

Grief, sorrow, anger, joy and laughter
are moods with inner feelings that always change.
They are not permanent…
even if the mind believes they are.

All emotions are subject to change,
arising and passing away.

Be the knower of this
and say to yourself…
Oh, that's just another impermanent
emotion showing up.

Notice it and acknowledge it
without grasping onto it.

Dreams…
They walk in our hearts
flow in our breath
and become part
of our thoughts.

Yet, we should not cling to the dream.
Find what is real…
what becomes of the dream?

The deep grief of loss
arrives from a love
that wishes to be shared.

Grasping onto desire is often based on false views.
Don't pick them up…
you can do that!

Notice when the heart is more expansive.
Beliefs and judgments about ourselves
and others drop away.

Try it out for six months.
Let me know what you think?

It takes courage to change how we process thoughts
when the minds demands on life are not being met.

Of course…
We will have to face the pain of how much and how
often, we've defended false assumptions.

Be kind toward yourself; the healing will come.

When trees of the forest shed their leaves
and become naked
there is an emptiness that happens.

Where there was no space before
there now is space.
What was unable to be seen earlier is now seen.

Thoughts should be considered the same as leaves
moving through their seasons.
They have their time and then pass away.

Why do humans continue clinging to thoughts
that have served their time and purpose
which cause self-inflicted pain?

The natural flow of nature is change…
The natural mind is one of openness…
The fear-mind clings to redemption for its anxieties.
The compassionate heart knows different.

Humans are of nature…
Give up your ideals of what you believe
it means to be human.
Your true nature will then emerge
through the emptiness that was once full.

It's in the continuous letting go
where a more ease of life can be found.

Notice the times when you do this and
perhaps a new spaciousness will be found.

What's it like always needing to be right?
An energy searching for a perfection that is nonexistent.
Does an experience of inner peace and calm happen?
I think not.
What might happen if we renounce this self-righteousness?

I'm tired of living in the delusion others create about
themselves...then place upon me.
I have enough of my own fallacies and illusions
that are exhausting.
Thank you very much!

Awakening II

*We must learn to nurture the mind of clarity, not make excuses
for the mind that wants to live in fogginess
and blame. Ignoring this truth never works in
helping anyone ultimately feel better.*

———————————

It's natural to grieve the loss of those who have been loved.
That's the fear and the path towards greater healing.

If the heart is to be liberated,
spiritual practice asks this of us.

When we awaken to a new truth or epiphany
our inner work is not turning it into a concrete reality.

Are we ready to see we are all connected
to the same source, not a separate self.

Ocean and river flow boundlessly
cradled in the arms of mud and sand.
Plants and trees find nourishment from the clouds of rain
...singing hallelujah!
All the while they are looking upward to the heavens
where the sky and father sun reside.

We grow and emerge from the womb of mother earth
as she nourishes our roots.
Insects, birds, reptiles and animals have no clue to be anything
other than god's ears and hands exploring life,
one moment at a time.

We must allow the heart to cradle our mind
in the center of its bosom
to free our thoughts like an artist's brush.

Paint and draw all that can be seen and touched.
Hear your sister wind sing out to you
the songs of distant lands.
Your brother nose will inhale all the ingredients
inside this stew called birth and death.

Learn to open your mouth as wide as possible.
Bite into this birthday cake called human consciousness
and chew every mouthful with gusto.
Taste each spice as it explodes with a new
story and spiritual epic.

Take your whole body and jump into this fire called life
burning itself back into ash and soil.

Realizing there never was a separation of earth and self
it was only a thought.

Grab this unseen umbilical cord.
Return it back to mother earth for her to suckle and nourish.
The heart and soul will free itself
to smile and laugh once again…
Opening up to cry away the sorrows long held by
the journey of a lost soul.

This separate self of fear will extinguish itself.
All that will be left is grandfather moon and grandmother stars
and the moving shadows of time awaiting, awaiting….
awaiting our presence.

No longer clinging to aversion
is to realize emptiness…
where the space for everything exists.

Wisdom: Not taking personal what is not you.
This will be difficult because what I'm proposing takes
away the sense of self we fight for and cling to.
This letting go may even feel like a struggle to keep
from dying...yet it's life-altering.
If only we could stop engaging with something
that is not even who we are.

Spirituality: To be in wholeness.
A completeness with the world as it is...not separate from it.

Nature

*We are of nature: Minerals, cells, atoms, protons,
neurons...Such as flowers, trees, sky, rocks, birds and earth.
Should we not stop believing we are other than nature?*

––––––––––––––––––––

Tall trees
wind blows
leaves touch the universe,
caressing mother earth.

As we touch you mother earth
we give thanks for your presence.
Allowing us to unfold into your awareness.

We offer gratitude…
To the great universal goddess of the cosmos
who brings substance and wholeness to all your children.

When we plant a seed, the flower will bloom.
How it will look or how tall it will grow, who knows?
No matter what…it will be quite glorious!

Hear the call of the Universe…
Your name will be sung from the highest mountains!

Can we be like nature?
A tree sheds its leaves
when they are no longer useful.

Can we shed thoughts that no longer serve us?
Allowing for the newness
of our own spring to come forth.

The forest acknowledges what it is and
does not strive to be anything other than a forest.

Why do humans strive not to be human
a struggle against what we are?

Recognize…
when striving becomes a self-imposed prison.

In our ability to live a joyful, compassionate life
we must learn to weather emotional upheavals.

Just as nature's weather patterns return to calm
the sun returns to shine after every storm.

Be the knower of storm experiences.
Conditions arise and pass away
throughout our lifetime..

Tell me…
why is it we struggle so much in knowing this?

The forest is a representation of our path
toward knowing and awakening.

When the forest is in full bloom
thick leaves are seen everywhere
all the various paths cannot be seen.

As the season turns
leaves fall from their branches.
Various colors will appear until
they wither and fall away.

Our view is no longer blocked, as
the various pathways are revealed.

What once seemed hidden and unknown,
becomes known and is now seen with the naked eye.

Just as we move deeper into self discovery
the unseen becomes seen.

What may have felt like a truth at one moment
suddenly vanishes.

To realize that all phenomena is in flux and changing is
one of the richest understandings within the mind of wisdom.

In nature…
plants and flowers grow strong from manure.
We are of nature too.

So the question arises…
"Why is it so difficult for us to wade in and see our own
manure…so that we also may grow
strong and expand ourselves?

A willingness to acknowledge the unpleasant
allows for a movement toward the pleasant.
A real connection to our ultimate potential.

Spiritual Reflections

The world we inhabit is our monastery.
The views we carry around live in the mind.
The path shows us the sorrows and joys of life.
The journey is our exploration in awakening to all this.

Awaken to the deep love of self
where the mind is sturdy and stable
understanding the frailty of the human condition.

Root out the causes and beliefs
which are untrue and not who you are.
Discover the inner spirit that is open and
free from being attached to false hopes.

Greet the compassionate heart of great wisdom
with open arms.
The fear of being loved
will no longer control you.

May we all move toward creating
the causes and conditions
which allow for tranquility
to arise in our lives.

May the twin pillars of joy and serenity be with us.
May we be touched by all that is…
the sun, the moon, the earth and beyond.

Allow the universal language of love and compassion
…inhabit the mind and actions of this body.

This human body of energy…
Is a mysterious, emotional, action-packed amusement park
taking us through a cornucopia of rides
swirling around, up and down
then floating on a cloud.

If we are not aware
we find ourselves
continuously experiencing
the same two or three familiar rides
over and over.

Throwing us for a loop
and stomach of queasiness.
Never noticing our death grip of clinging
to just these few experiences.

As if there is nothing else
happening or going on around us
in this amusement park of life!

I am the one who knows
the secret that lies deeply inside.

You who thought there was only birth.
You thought there was no aging or sickness.

There was only the joy of play…
this delusion where life is only one way.

Oh how I weep for what could not be seen…
The ultimate journey had been forgotten.

Where birth becomes flesh,
flesh becomes life…life returns back to earth.

We must not forget about wonder and grace.

The nourishing of faith reveals
the shadow of the soul that
lies behind us at all times.

Gaze into the grass where goodness grows
and the children play at our feet.

In time, it will be remembered again…
there is none other than cause and effect.

Why is this so difficult to see?

A Stroll In The Forest ...

It was a warm autumn afternoon as I sauntered into the New
England forest that day. Soft greens, warm golden yellows,
saffron and orange rust-colored leaves all about.
You could hear the crunch as my feet lifted and settled.
Oh my, the mind ablaze in joy and wonder.
Where and how did such beauty arise!
And it found me, of all people...
or perhaps we found each other?
Without notice a light breeze entered the forest.
Suddenly, the light lemon yellow leaves took flight from their
branches.
Butterflies they were in the sky!
Gliding on the wind
right before my very own eyes, and they said...
"Come join us and be free."
And guess what? My mind actually agreed!
My body could feel it, I really am free.
And without notice tears of joy expressed...
"don't forget about us."
They too took flight down the cheeks, past the smile,
washing my clean white shirt with moisture.
I continued on that lovely afternoon, strolling here and
strolling there.
Stumbling over stones and the tree roots
of my new found friends.
And whenever I paused...the forest was silent.

There were no stories of right or wrong here.
Just the pure essence of the present moment…
the silence within.
It's in all of us you know?
Though it only happens when we pause
and open our ears to it.

As I came to the end of this delightful walk
I strode out into the open green pasture
and there she was…the sun gazing down on me.
Drenching me in purity, light and goodness.

Well, the next thing I did, which I do believe
was quite rational and sane.
I looked upward into the infinite blue sky and I asked…
God, how could this have happened to me?
How could I be the one that receives so much joy?

And, you know what? She answered…
"The heart knows everything and everything is the heart."

Conclusion

When I describe the taste of spiritual life
my flavor will be slightly different from yours.
Attached to thinking we must all experience life
the same way is a path of false view.

If we are to stop creating a world that causes
a war against itself, we must standup to the war
inside ourselves and say no more to the "stingy mind."

Remember…you can return anytime
to any page…pause and reflect.

Reflective Poems On Loss

I Didn't Know

I wanted to say…though I didn't
I wanted to tell you…though I forgot
Can I do this alone…I had to
Waiting for the right moment…it never appeared
I knew to go for a walk…yet I couldn't
My eyes said enough…yet the tears weren't finished
I wanted to meet you…though you were a no-show
The experience of loss had taken a form
Memories invade like a shadow reaching for light
You are here and you are not here
Grasping for you makes your absence more real
I wasn't quite finished and yet there's no choice
Time can feel limited…even after many years
I'm waiting for the limits of my heart to ease
Not from the pain though from forgiveness
I must remember again and again and again
The body of clay is limited even as I wish for more.

Alone With Loss

I grieved your loss
Alone…alone…alone, I grieved.
Everyone said they were here for me.
And yet, when I looked around, there were no faces.
Life, you lied to me…
Or so I thought.
The message… "Don't worry dear, everything will work out."
Well, it didn't work out. Even you died and left me.
You died, and before you, others died.
And after you others will continue to die.
Who is left…who is left?
There is no one, not even me.
Yes, you see, I will also die…and the others will be alone.
How can it be any other way?
People care and we all wish another well, yet...
How could anyone know what's inside?
What was shared.
It was special, it was ours….no one knew.
Alone…alone…I grieved.
I did my best to be there for you.

Yet, I did not know the secret then that life held.
How could I have known?
My grief, your grief...our collective grief.
Loss will always come...
Never afraid to hide its face.
It's mine, just as it belongs to everyone.
Touching what is...we walk together.
Watering this grief one more time...
So the flowers may begin to bloom once again
while lying dormant, waiting for the spring.
Alone, alone...life begins to flourish from the unknown.

No More Hiding

I went out looking for a poem on grieving
though you were nowhere to be found
amongst the many words of loss and grief.

You see I wanted something different this time.
Not the usual prose of open-hearted everything will be ok
kindness.

I wanted the stirring of angst to arise,
no mushy wariness here.
I'm angry, I'm tired, I'm depressed,
I'm miserable, I'm confused.
This sucks, how could this be…
Life, you are torturing me!

Yes, those are the words I needed to hear.
Honest heartfelt, non-understanding, the mind saying…
I'll never get through this…that's the type of recognition
I'm talking about.

This is my truth, nothing flaky going on here.
Only heartfelt shakiness, losing my grounding…
grieving and heaving.

Something happens here, when I notice how this body reacts in
such a way.

I quit hiding. I come out of the dark, that dank coldness
of thinking loss should be anything other than this.

A lousy, miserable, gut-wrenching happens in the changing of the guard of life.

It will not and cannot be the same as it was, never again.
Grief makes me recognize myself without you.

I'm tired of being numb to this grieving.
I want to feel the strength of its tsunami.

Perhaps some of you may think I'm nuts for inviting all this in.
Yet, I've come to learn it's the only place I can come to terms with the present.

This place of misery allows me to notice when grieving pauses and softens.

Then once again I smile, as your face and memory
lay upon the warm soft cushion of my heart.

Where you and I rest together…as the sun sets.
Until it arises again into another day of grieving and healing.

My thanks to Ileana LaBergere who helped in pulling together the many reflections I've written over the years.

To my friend Cindy Lutz for her editing skills and continued support in asking me questions. A big shout out of appreciation to Carla Dal Mas for the book-cover design and Paula Egan <paulaegan.com> for her beautiful book cover artwork and the leaf images between each reflection.

To Grant Young taking time to review the book, share at the dinner table with his family to discuss, then write the preface. There are many others not named here whom deserve much gratitude in offering their words or critiquing support as I honed this book toward completion.

ABOUT THE AUTHOR

Rik Center began a mindful meditation practice in the late 1980s. He has served as a Buddhist Interfaith Chaplain at San Francisco General Hospital and at CPMC/Sutter Health Hospitals in San Francisco where he presently sits on the Professional Advisory Group for Spiritual Care. Rik is Cofounder of the nonprofit the Mindfulness Care Center, through which he teaches a variety of mindfulness meditation classes, plus workshops on dissolving stress and unresolved anxiety. He's developed a unique mindfulness and unresolved traumatic anxiety program called The DEER Program: Developing Emotional Embodied Resiliency.

Rik has an ongoing private practice working one-on-one with clients that focuses on healing high levels of stress, unresolved traumatic anxiety and PTSD along with offering grief and spiritual counseling. He's a member of the United States Association Of Body Psychotherapy.

CPSIA information can be obtained
at www.ICGtesting.com
Printed in the USA
BVHW032313210120
569971BV00029B/555